D1287753

TO THE RESCUE!

THE HISTORY OF EMERGENCY VEHICLES

Peter Lafferty and David Jefferis

Franklin Watts
New York   London   Toronto   Sydney

Illustrated by
Robert Burns
Chris Forsey
Doug Harker
Ron Jobson
Michael Roffe

Photographs supplied by
Norman Barrett
Dennis Specialist
    Vehicles Ltd
David Jefferis
London Fire Brigade

Technical consultant
Patrick Devereaux

© 1990 Franklin Watts

Franklin Watts Inc.
387 Park Avenue South
New York, NY 10016

Printed in Belgium

All rights reserved

Library of Congress Cataloging-in-Publication data

Lafferty, Peter
To the rescue : the history of emergency vehicles / Peter Lafferty and David Jefferis.
p. cm – – (Wheels)
Includes bibliographical references
Summary: Follows the development of emergency vehicles, such as ambulances and fire engines.
ISBN 0–531–14085–7
1. Emergency vehicles – Juvenile literature. [1. Emergency vehicles.] I. Jefferis. David. II. Title. III. Series: Lafferty, Peter. Wheels.
TL236.8.L33 1990
629, 225 – dc20

89-21541
CIP
AC

TO THE RESCUE!

Contents

Introduction

This book is about the vehicles that are used by the fire, police and ambulance services.

If someone needs assistance, an emergency telephone call is usually all it takes to get help fast. It wasn't always like this though, and until today's high-tech vehicles were developed, if you were in a dangerous situation, help might take a long time to arrive.

The first fire fighters were volunteers, passing buckets of water from hand to hand. Fire pumps, developed in the 1700s, improved things, though human muscle still provided the power. By the 19th century, the newly-invented steam engine enabled fire fighters to successfully tackle really big blazes. Today's machinery ranges from cross-country fire tenders to giant turntable ladders for rescuing people from high buildings. Fighting a blaze is a complex and skilled job, carried out by professional crews.

Ambulances started as little more than covered carts, pulled by horses. Today's vehicles carry a wide range of medical equipment, allowing crews to give efficient treatment to anything from fuel burns to broken bones on the spot, thereby keeping patients alive until arrival at hospital.

Police vehicles are mostly based on existing cars and light trucks, with many added extras. These can include items such as sirens and searchlights, powerful engines and strengthened suspension systems.

◁ Emergency crews work at the site of a crashed airliner. Major events like this bring all three emergency services together as a disaster control team. Fire-fighters battle the blaze and ambulance crews deal with the injured. Police control the flow of people and traffic in the area.

Emergency vehicles

Here are three examples from the hundreds of different types of emergency vehicle in use around the world. Police cars and ambulances are mostly based on standard saloons and light trucks, fitted out with any extra equipment or special bodywork needed for the job.

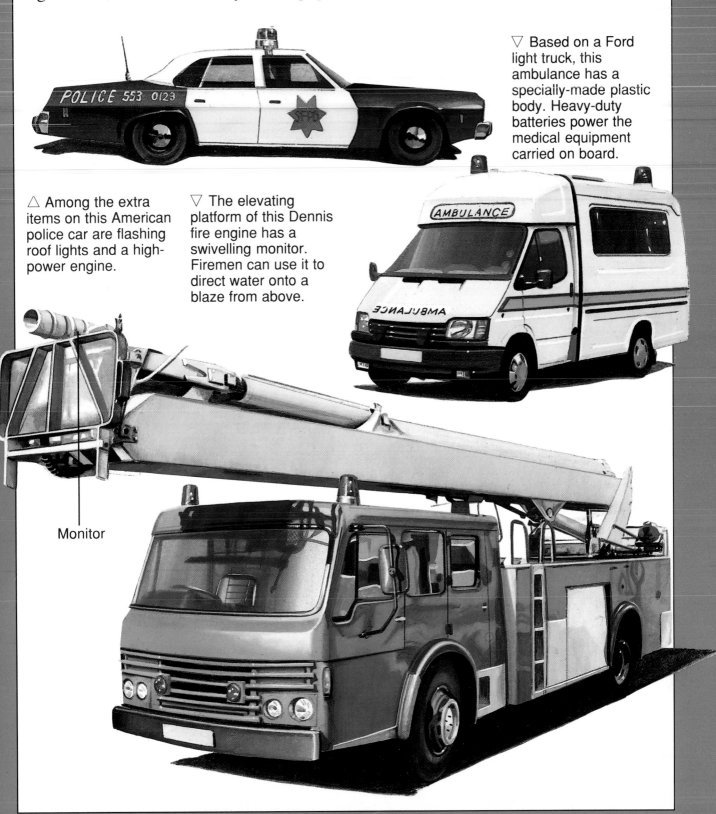

▽ Based on a Ford light truck, this ambulance has a specially-made plastic body. Heavy-duty batteries power the medical equipment carried on board.

△ Among the extra items on this American police car are flashing roof lights and a high-power engine.

▽ The elevating platform of this Dennis fire engine has a swivelling monitor. Firemen can use it to direct water onto a blaze from above.

POLICE 553 0123

AMBULANCE

Monitor

The first fire engines

The earliest fire engines were simple pumps, which could squirt small amounts of water at fires. Though such devices had been used as far back as Roman times, the first machine known to be designed especially for fire fighting was invented by Englishman Roger Jones in 1625. According to reports of the time, ten men using his machine could pump water as quickly as 500 people using buckets alone. In 1721, London engineer Richard Newsham invented the first really successful fire engine. Two hand-operated pumps were placed in a water tank mounted on wheels. The pumps supplied a steady stream of water that was sprayed out of a brass nozzle mounted on top. The success of this machine encouraged Newsham to develop the design further, and in a few years he had a range of six fire engines for sale, the biggest having a tank capacity of 757 liters (170 gal). It could send a jet of water more than 36 meters (120 ft), though the tank needed a refill after a minute's pumping.

At this time, there were no fire brigades as we know them today. Fire engines were usually kept at the local church and volunteers fought the flames. The first real fire brigades were formed by fire insurance companies, which, for a fee, offered to protect their customers' houses from destruction. The insurance brigades were great rivals, racing to reach a fire first. Once at a blaze, firemen would check to see if the building belonged to one of their customers. If not, they might leave it to burn or make only halfhearted attempts to save it. The better brigades preferred to put out fires in the hope that owners would take out insurance to guard against future disasters.

Brawling between brigades was common. Rushing to a blaze, firemen often tried to run each other's machines off the road or into a wall. At a fire, they fought over who used the water supply. And when some brigades speeded things up by using horses to pull their engines, rivals accused them of cheating.

◁ According to this advertisement of 1728, Richard Newsham's engines could be used for other purposes than mere fire fighting, for which a "constant stream" of water was promised. When there was no fire, the engine's owner could use it "at pleasure, to water gardens like falling rain."

△ Much of London was razed to the ground in the Great Fire of 1666, which burned for three days. Among the few pieces of fire fighting equipment were these fire squirts, which pumped a bucketful of water at a time. The early fire pump, shown top right, was mounted on wooden runners.

▽ By the 19th century, pumps and hose reels were mounted on wheels, though they were still pulled by people. Here, teams of firemen race to be first at a blaze in 1854.

Steamers

The first fire pump to be powered by a steam engine was built by the London firm of Braithwaite and Ericsson in 1829. Though the machine could put out a jet of water nearly 30m (100ft) long, its power was more than matched by the strength of its opposition. Many firemen claimed the new machine was too heavy and awkward to handle. Others didn't want to lose the money they were paid to work pumps by hand. Just four more Braithwaite steamers were built, including one that ended up in Russia. For the time being, firemen still pumped water using their muscles.

In the years that followed, more steam engines were developed, and in 1840 the first self-propelled steamer was built by American engineer Paul Hodge. The age of steam had truly arrived, yet lots of firemen still refused to accept it, and many spectacular competitions were held between steamers and hand-pumpers,

including an epic match held in 1853.

When the contest started, the hand pump team went straight into the lead. In moments they were putting out a huge jet of water, while the steamer wheezed away, slowly building up pressure. But as the minutes passed, the hand pumpers started to tire and eventually had to stop. Gasping from the effort, they stood back to watch the steam engine. By now, it was roaring away at full power and sent out a massive water jet. Then its operators overwhelmed the hand pump team by turning on another set of water jets to show what their steamer could achieve when opened up to the limit.

In 1865, a fire at Barnum's Museum in New York showed what steam equipment could do in a real disaster. Though lots of equipment and many animals were lost in the flames, much of the museum was saved by the firemen and their puffing steamers.

△ A fireman tackles a crazed tiger in the huge Barnum's Museum fire of 1865. After this, New York built up a full-time fire department, which included over 80 steam pumps and 500 men.

▽ The 1899 Merryweather Fire King became the pride of many brigades, including that of Brighton in 1903. The Fire King's powerful steam engine drove the wheels as well as the pump.

△ New York's firemen go to the rescue in the 1860s. As the steam pump clatters along, a stoker feeds the boiler to build up maximum pressure. Hose reel and ladders are pulled on separate wagons.

Speed and power

The internal-combustion engine was developed in the 1880s. This new engine, similar in basic principles to the ones we use in today's vehicles, was smaller and more powerful for its weight than the old steamers. In a few years, early automobiles became an increasingly common sight on the roads. Soon they were joined by trucks and the first motorized fire engines.

In 1904, the Finchley fire brigade of London took delivery of the latest in motor-driven fire engines. Its water pump was powered by the same engine that turned the driving wheels, a world first. The pump, of simple centrifugal design, could send 1,138 liters (250 gal) a minute through a pair of fire fighting hoses. The great advantage of using an internal-combustion engine for pumping was that full power came on immediately. There was no waiting for a steam engine to build up pressure. Finchley's motorized fire engine scored well in other ways too, especially in its speed and power. In an emergency, a good driver could hit 32 km/h (20 mph) on smooth roads. The fire engine was a good hauler, carrying a heavy load that included an extending ladder, water hoses and medical equipment. It also had another pump, to back up the main motor pumper. This used chemicals to make carbon dioxide, the gas used in carbonated drinks. Gas pressure forced water along a hose until the chemicals were finished.

Once they found out how useful the new motorized vehicles were, fire services around the world started to adopt them. Demand for horses dropped rapidly as new fire stations were built, so large stables were no longer necessary. The age of horse and steam power was ending.

∇ Finchley fire brigade's motorized fire engine of 1904.

△ These German Mercedes fire engines, of 1907 (left), and 1909, had hose reels mounted at the back, ready for use.

▽ Twin rear wheels took the weight of the equipment carried by this American LaFrance appliance of 1917. Like other early engines, the crew sat in the open.

▷ The centrifugal pump contains a fanlike impeller (**1**). Water is fed through an inlet pipe (**2**), and spun outward with great force by the spinning fan blades (**3**). The water is hurled out of the pump through the outlet pipe (**4**).

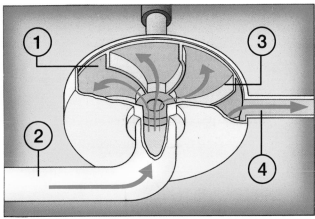

Towering inferno

In the early 1900s, several disasters proved that better equipment was needed for emergency work.

One blaze destroyed a Chicago theater in the United States on December 30, 1903. Although the building was designed with safety in mind, hundreds of lives were lost because of some simple planning mistakes. On the ground floor, fire exits jammed shut against the crush of terrified theatergoers trying to get out. Upstairs, the theater had no outside emergency stairs. Many people, trapped on the upper floors, fell to their doom rather than face the searing flames. Rescuers could do little to help when they arrived, because space outside was too tight to put up high ladders next to the theater.

After this and other disasters, safety standards and fire fighting equipment were both improved. Extending ladders that could reach the upper floors of buildings from confined spaces were introduced.

Some were mounted on wheels for easy positioning. Others were attached to turntables on fire engines.

Today, the most advanced type of aerial equipment is the snorkel. This uses a two or three-section extending boom, with a platform at the top. Water pipes are built into the boom, so fire fighters can tackle a blaze using a monitor. The platform can also be used as a rescue cage to pluck people to safety. Other plus points for the snorkel include speed and safety. It takes just a few seconds to get a snorkel team up and fighting a fire, with no danger to them from collapsing walls or falling timber. Fire fighters can control their position using an instrument panel on the platform, but there is a duplicate set of controls at ground level, just in case there are problems up above. To keep things cool, a water curtain can be sprayed from pipes mounted under the platform floor.

◁ Mack is one of the oldest fire equipment manufacturers. The pumper shown here is a 1970s model, with a monitor mounted over the cab. In many fires, water from the hoses can wreck interiors untouched by the flames. Damage control teams back up the fire fighters by carrying out salvage work. They cover things with waterproof sheets, open up drains to allow water to flow away, clear floors of broken glass and other debris.

▷ Before heavy duty appliances like this snorkel get to the scene, "first aid" vehicles have usually arrived. They carry basic fire fighting equipment for controlling a blaze in its early stages. In this picture, Hong Kong firemen gain control of a blaze. Support jacks are extended on either side of the snorkel to keep the boom steady.

▽ When a main water supply hydrant is available, getting water to a fire is a simple job.
1 The hydrant is opened. A suction hose is run out and attached to it.
2 The other end of the hose is connected to the pump's inlet valve.
3 A delivery hose is attached to the pump's output valve. The hose is run out to the fire.
4 A nozzle is attached to the hose end. Water is turned on at the hydrant. The pump is then switched on and the fire fighters can attack the blaze.

① ② ③ ④

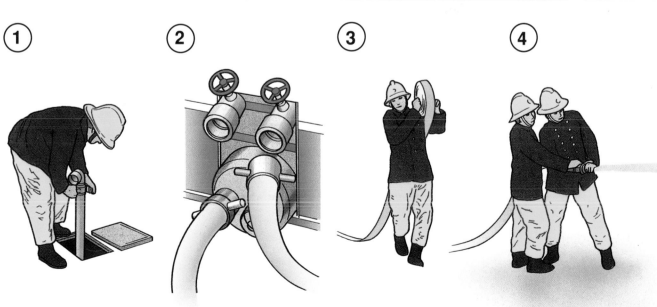

13

Airport alert

△ Emergency vehicles take control of an aircraft fire, spraying foam to kill the flames.

The most hazardous parts of any air flight are at takeoff and landing. About three quarters of all incidents happen on or near the runway. Airliners carry huge quantities of fuel – a Boeing 747 holds 200,000 liters (44,000 gal) or more on a long flight – so a plane is a potential fireball in an emergency.

Every airport has a fleet of fire and medical equipment standing by in case of trouble, including heavy duty water and foam tankers, ambulances, and cutting and lifting gear. Powerful floodlights are used for night work. Racing ahead of the main crash fleet are RIVs – rapid intervention vehicles – which can control a blaze within minutes, containing the fire until the bigger fire trucks get to the scene. Light rescue

units carry fire fighters wearing aluminized heat-resistant clothing.

Though emergency crews go on alert at least once a day at a busy airport, most incidents are minor. A pilot may have a hydraulic failure or a cockpit warning light may come on unexpectedly. More seriously, a main undercarriage leg might not extend properly, as happened to a Delta Air Lines flight in March 1988. The plane, carrying seven crew and 69 passengers, made its approach to Portland airport with no left main wheels locked down.

Standard procedure in cases like this is for the foam tankers to lay a thick carpet of foam on the runway to suppress any sparks when metal hits the concrete. Emergency

crews then go to stand-by positions near the runway and wait for the crippled plane to land. Even before it has stopped moving, fire trucks hurry to the plane. More foam is sprayed onto the wings, where most of the remaining fuel is stored. Dry powder is squirted onto local hot spots such as the tires and wheel bays. Fire fighters may wear breathing gear when both foam and powder are being used, as they give off poison fumes when mixed together. Rubber chutes pop out from the doors and passengers slide down to the ground, where medical teams take care of them. The people on the Delta flight were lucky – all emergency procedures worked as planned and no one was killed.

▷ Fire crews practice constantly. Main water is unavailable for most airfield fires, so engines carry their own supplies. A big vehicle can carry about 10,000 liters (2,200 gal) of water, which can be mixed to make foam.

Carrying the sick

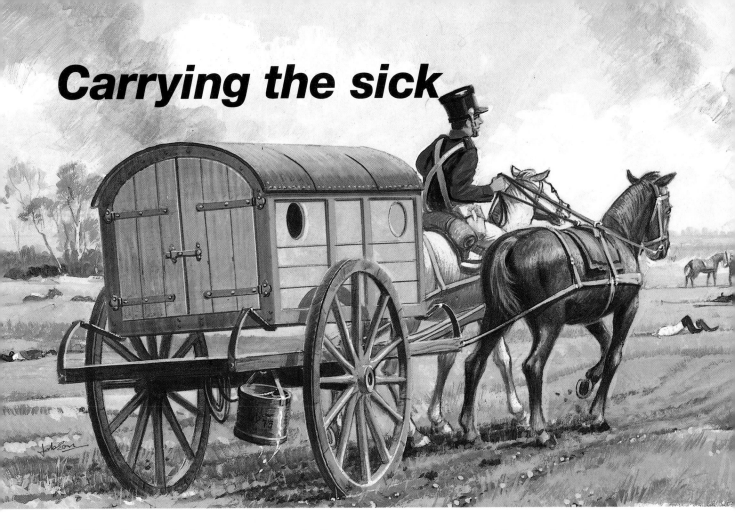

The first ambulances were made for military use, to carry wounded soldiers from battlefields. In about 1790, two French army surgeons developed a horse-drawn "ambulance volante," the flying ambulance. Although it was little more than a covered cart, it could carry two wounded men on stretchers and had a set of surgical instruments on board.

In June 1859, Swiss banker Henri Dunant was traveling in Italy. He was appalled to see the results of the battle of Solferino, fought between the forces of Austria, France and Sardinia. On the battle field were thousands of wounded soldiers. Those with leg wounds managed to use sticks or rifles as crutches; many others lay in agony. Dunant did what he could, helped by the local people, using wagons and carts as ambulances. Later he formed the famous international Red Cross organization. It continues to this day, helping the sick and wounded in times of conflict.

One of the main problems with these early ambulances was giving the patients a smooth ride – a bumpy ride for someone who is wounded is not the best road to recovery! By the 1870s, Red Cross ambulances had metal springs to improve comfort during the ride.

The first peacetime ambulances were used in the 1880s to carry people with smallpox. The vehicles were painted black and completely enclosed to prevent the spread of the disease. The poor ventilation meant that patients often ran the risk of near suffocation before reaching the hospital.

Another early ambulance was an experimental machine of 1892. This used a pair of side by side bicycles, linked by metal tubes, with a stretcher mounted between them. Fit riders could reach 16 km/h (10 mph).

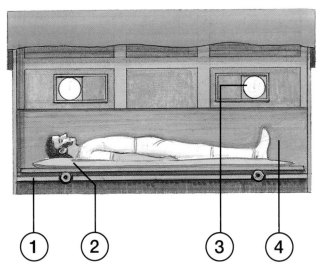

(1) (2) (3) (4)

◁ △ The flying
ambulance at work
after a battle in the
1790s. Inside, its
features included:
1 Two frames, one for
each patient. Rollers
enabled them to be
slid through the rear
doors.
2 Frame has a

horsehair mattress
and a leather covered
pillow.
3 Windows with sliding
shutters for ventilation.
4 The ambulance
sides were partly
padded in case
patients rolled off their
frames. Pockets held
surgical supplies.

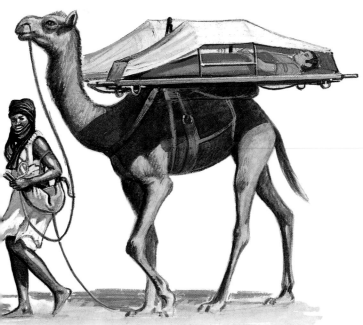

△ This two-person
camel ambulance was
used by the French in
North Africa in the
1850s. The wounded
soldiers lay on either

side of the camel's
body. Thick buffalo
hide straps kept
everything in place.
Cushions made the
ride comfortable.

△ In 1860,
ambulance barrows
were used by the
British Army in China.
The barrows were
designed to be pulled

by horses, if any were
available. If not, local
Chinese laborers were
pushed into service,
to do the job
rickshaw style.

Ambulance progress

Crossley 20/25

Ford Model T

Ambulance design took a giant step forward during World War I. With a casualty rate at the battlefront in France running at 40,000 or more killed and wounded a day, there was a huge demand for a speedy way to get wounded soldiers to hospitals based behind the lines.

One of the best ambulances was based on the Ford Model T car, first introduced in 1908. Open-top tourers were used as ambulances to begin with, then special bodies of wood and canvas were built onto the Model T's running gear. Unfortunately, these bodies were not quite long enough for standard army-issue stretchers, so holes were drilled into the tailgates to let the stretcher handles poke through. Blankets were stuffed into the gaps to prevent drafts.

The method of producing special ambulance bodywork, fitted onto existing car or truck running gear, continues to this day, with everything from Ford Transit vans to Cadillac limousines being equipped for medical work. Special bodies are often made of light but strong fiberglass, while interiors are usually finished in plastic materials. These are easy to clean and disinfect, keeping surfaces free of germs, which is an important factor when carrying sick or injured people.

An ambulance often carries enough specialized equipment to allow the crew, usually a driver and attendant, to use the vehicle as a mobile hospital. Basic essentials include a stretcher trolley, blankets, surgical dressings, splints to support broken bones, and drugs of various kinds. Other equipment can include a suction device to clear breathing passages, a piped oxygen supply and a heart-condition monitor.

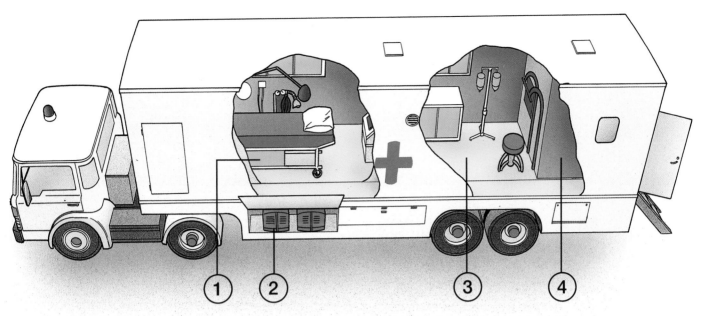

(1) (2) (3) (4)

◁ In World War I, many women joined the war effort as nurses and often as ambulance drivers, in charge of such vehicles as the ones shown here.

△ In the 1970s, this mobile hospital was used to treat accident victims at Grand Prix racetracks. It included a main operating theatre (**1**), portable power generators (**2**), a room for examination and minor surgery (**3**), and a reception area (**4**). Equipment included a refrigerated blood bank and a heart reviving machine.

▽ Ambulance crew demonstrates heart resuscitation equipment. Their task is to ensure a person's survival until full hospital facilities are reached.

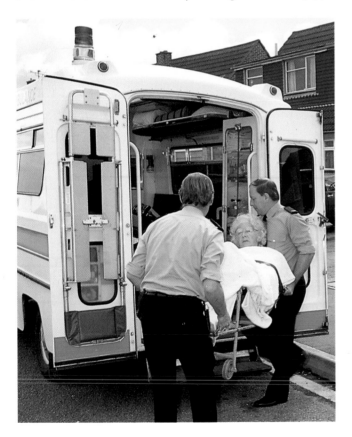

△ When patients are too sick to walk, then wheeled stretchers can be used to get them aboard an ambulance.

Police vehicles

The crews of police vehicles work as part of a highly trained team, in touch with headquarters by radio. Important jobs include fighting crime, assisting the public, and traffic patrols.

Like ambulances, police vehicles are based mostly on existing machines, available from the production lines of the world's auto manufacturers. However, a typical patrol car has a range of features and equipment that makes it very different from the car on which it is based.

The engine is modified to give more power, for better acceleration and a higher top speed, both important factors if the car is involved in a highway pursuit. To cope with the extra power, high-performance tires are added. A modified suspension system gives a firmer ride, reducing body roll when cornering hard. A heavy duty battery copes with extra electrical loads, such as flashing lights on the roof and a loud siren.

Inside the patrol car, easy-to-clean, durable vinyl covers the seats. Other equipment includes a powerful two-way radio for communications with police controllers, searchlights, first-aid kit and a fire extinguisher. The car is finished off with a special police paint scheme on the bodywork.

◁ The first police vehicles were pulled by horses. Here a police van stops to pick up a group of prisoners from Clerkenwell prison, London, in 1862. A modern police van may look ordinary, but the body may be fitted with a powerful motor. The British Sherpa police van has a V8 engine, enough to hit 160 km/h (100 mph) or more if necessary.

△ Police forces use the most modern vehicles they can, often trying machines out for an experimental period. In 1935, this Chrysler Airflow was an advanced car, with front-wheel drive and smoothly styled bodywork.

▷ Most police cars, including this New York model, only stay on the force for two to three years before they are replaced. After their tour of duty, most patrol cars are sold to private buyers after police equipment has been removed.

Traffic patrol

The job of traffic police is to keep roads free from traffic jams and to see that drivers don't break the law. Traffic police deal with accidents and problems such as spilled truckloads on the highway.

Police control centers are in charge. If an accident occurs, patrol cars are sent to the scene of the crash to direct operations, to ensure that medical teams can get through quickly, to keep traffic out of the way and to organize removal of the wreckage. As well as emergency work, traffic police carry out many routine jobs, such as monitoring speeding vehicles and inspecting others that look unsafe.

There are a number of machines that can be used to check vehicle speeds. The radar gun is very common. The operator aims the gun at a target car and presses a button as it passes two landmarks. The gun then computes the car's speed, displaying it on a digital readout. Even more efficient than a radar gun is Gatso, which takes a picture of a vehicle as it passes an unmarked police car. The vehicle's speed, the time and the date are imprinted on the photograph. Gatso is used in several countries, including Holland, Germany and Australia. Other countries, including Britain, are planning to introduce it.

When questioned about catching speeding drivers, few police officers admit to being interested in anything but safety. Road accidents cause many casualties – in 1987 there were 10,742 deaths in France alone – and the police are on the front line, from dealing with the wreckage to informing the relatives of the victims.

◁ Many of the same driving mistakes are made again and again, such as driving too fast in foggy and wet weather. These mistakes can cause road accidents that waste time, money and lives. In such conditions, braking distances need to be much further than usual. Sharp braking in the wet is all too likely to lead to a skid – and an accident.

Police vehicles around the world

Here are some of the world's favorite police vehicles. The Range Rover is particularly popular. Its high seating position gives good visibility, and the four-wheel drive system makes it very safe in bad weather. Range Rovers can also be driven safely off road when necessary.

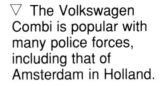

▽ The Volkswagen Combi is popular with many police forces, including that of Amsterdam in Holland.

△ A Moscow police car. This vehicle, a version of an old Fiat design, has a roofrack holding a flashing blue emergency warning light, and a pair of loudspeaker horns.

◁ In West Germany, police patrol the high-speed autobahns in fast cars such as this Porsche sports model. Big numbers on the top surfaces can be read from the air so police helicopter crews can identify the car.

▽ Apart from being a fast police cruiser, the Range Rover is powerful enough to tow wrecked cars off the road.

△ The squat French Citroen looks like a square can made of corrugated iron. However, it has been a popular machine, used by the police of several countries. This one belongs to the Paris police department.

Emergency, year 2010

Despite our best efforts to avoid disasters, accidents still happen, and will continue to do so in the foreseeable future. Here are some of the vehicles that may be developed to provide emergency cover in the early years of the 21st century.

The police cruiser has four-wheel drive to give increased road grip and better driver control in bad weather. Pursuit lights are built into the roof section, reducing air drag to improve both power consumption and top speed. The car also features advanced computer equipment to track and identify suspect vehicles. A satellite link enables officers in the car to check on information stored in computer files at police headquarters. An update of present systems, the equipment can check on the criminals of other countries too, if necessary.

The fire fighting group is a possible support system to bring major disasters in city and industrial areas under control. The big fire truck is equipped with an extension platform that can be remote controlled to spray water or foam on high-intensity fires. Despite its size, the truck is easy to maneuver – its body is split into several sections, so it can wriggle around corners like a caterpillar. The fire fighting robots come in two types, manned, and fully automatic. Both can penetrate fires to rescue people trapped by the heat and flames.

The ambulance is a self-contained medical center, designed for on the spot treatments. Critically ill patients are placed in emergency pods, and are airlifted to a hospital by a helicopter air ambulance.

▽ In action against a future blaze, two robots await orders to enter the roaring inferno. The rescue robots can walk into the hottest fires, carrying people to safety in refrigerated compartments. The heavy duty fire trucks smother the flames with chemical foam. A survivor has been placed in a survival pod.

▷ The police pursuit vehicle includes these advanced features:
1 Automatic video camera keeps visual track of target vehicles. **2** Electric motors give a pollution-free ride.
3 Electronic antenna links to a satellite for computer and video communications.
4 Rear display can be changed to read any message.

Rescue machines

These vehicles cover more than a century of progress in the development of emergency equipment.

△ In 1889, the first of three electric fire cars ran on the streets of Paris. Each carried six firemen at a speed of 19 km/h (12 mph).

△ There was such a shortage of motor ambulances in World War I that some people lent their cars for the job. This open tourer was converted for Red Cross use.

△ This 1980s ambulance is based on a Range Rover. A longer version is also made, with a wide loading door by the rear wheel.

▷ In 1934, the Vienna fire service in Austria used this six wheel fire engine, capable of crossing rough country on the way to a fire.

△ In 1940, the California Highway Patrol (CHP) used Mercury patrol cars like this, painted in the CHP black and white colors.

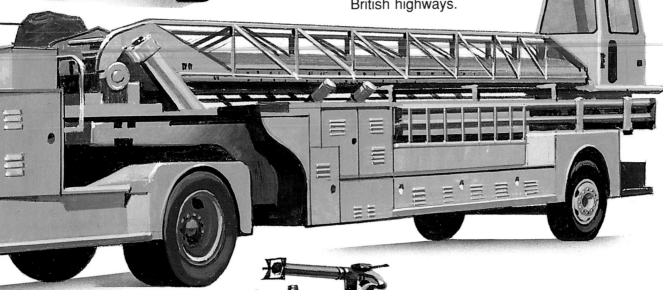

◁ The 1990 Ford Sapphire RS Cosworth is one of the fastest patrol cars in the world. It can top 240 km/h (150 mph). This one is used to patrol British highways.

△ This Leyland Cub was made in 1940. Its ladder could be moved around on the pair of big wheels at the back.

△ The massive 1975 Seagrave mounts a ladder for rescues from high buildings. A tillerman sits in the cab at the back, steering the vehicle's rear end safely around tight city corners.

▷ This 1980s Oshkosh is built to fight aircraft fires. The huge wheels allow the machine to cross soft ground.

Facts and records

Here are some interesting facts and figures, ideas and machines from the world of emergency vehicles.

The pictures below show pieces of early fire fighting equipment.

1 The 1881 "Quick Hitch" was designed to overcome one of the problems of using horses. Normally, the animals had to be kept in their harnesses, attached to the fire engine all day if necessary. With the Quick Hitch, horses could be kept in a yard nearby, where they were free to walk about. When an emergency call came, they were backed into position, the harness dropped on and buckled up. In just moments, the engine could be on its way.

2 The "Quadricycle Hose Carrier" of 1885. Armed with hoses and hydrant connectors, four men could pedal to a fire, connect up to the main water supply and often get a blaze under control without having to call out the main fire engine.

3 These 1920s firemen are using an early type of breathing apparatus to enable them to enter a smoke-filled building in safety. Smoke and fumes are as big a danger as flames and heat. Burning furniture, particularly if made of rubber and plastic materials, often gives off poison gases, which can make people unconscious long before they are in any danger from the fire itself.

4 Flame-resistant clothing is often an essential requirement. The suit shown here dates from the 1930s. In it, a fireman could stay in fierce heat for several minutes, peering through a fireproof glass visor.

When the first law enforcement agencies were formed, policemen rode horses to chase criminals. Toward the end of the 19th century, police became mechanized when they started using bicycles. After World War I, police chiefs started using cars instead of the traditional pony and trap. In the 1950s and 1960s, policemen on foot patrols were often replaced with fewer men, in cars, to cover a wider area. In recent years however, the bicycle has made a comeback in some countries, as cops on bicycles are thought to be more approachable

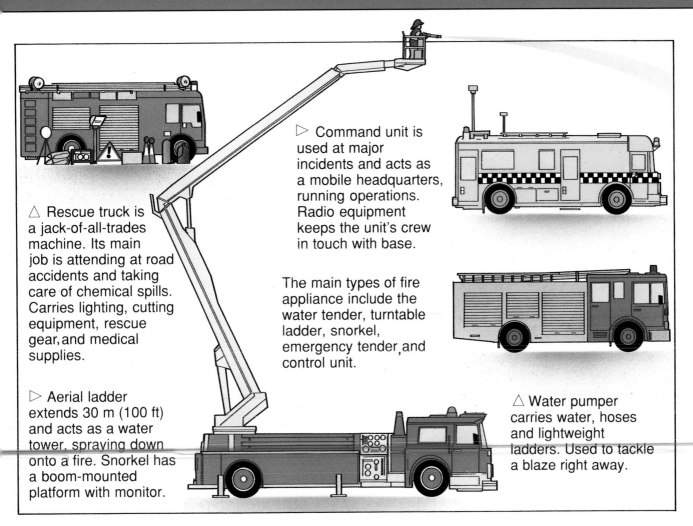

△ Rescue truck is a jack-of-all-trades machine. Its main job is attending at road accidents and taking care of chemical spills. Carries lighting, cutting equipment, rescue gear, and medical supplies.

▷ Command unit is used at major incidents and acts as a mobile headquarters, running operations. Radio equipment keeps the unit's crew in touch with base.

The main types of fire appliance include the water tender, turntable ladder, snorkel, emergency tender, and control unit.

▷ Aerial ladder extends 30 m (100 ft) and acts as a water tower, spraying down onto a fire. Snorkel has a boom-mounted platform with monitor.

△ Water pumper carries water, hoses and lightweight ladders. Used to tackle a blaze right away.

to the public. Police officers on mountain bikes can chase criminals in places where cars can't go. Mountain bike patrolmen in Seattle, Washington, have had success fighting the drug dealers in that city. In the words of one officer, "We ride through potholes, mud and dirt." In a chase, officers can "... dump the bike and hit the ground running. We haven't lost a suspect yet – or a bike."

The world's worst fire in a single building was in China in 1845. In May of that year, 1,670 people died as Canton's theater burned to the ground.

Ambulances are used for routine "journeys" as well as accident and emergency work. In a large city such as London, there are 8,000 or more routine journeys each day, mainly to take people to outpatient clinics in hospitals. Emergency calls are fewer, but still large in big cities. In London, ambulance crews go out on about 1,500 emergency calls a day.

On Christmas Day 1971, the Hotel Daeyungak in Seoul, South Korea, caught fire. Despite the best efforts of the emergency services, 162 people perished in the flames and smoke.

The emergency services try their best to keep road casualties to a minimum, but it's an uphill and never-ending task. In 1975, researchers estimated that a staggering total of 25 million people had lost their lives in road accidents since the invention of the automobile.

Bush fires are one of Australia's biggest enemies, often raging across a 30 km (19 mi) front, moving faster than walking pace. A firebreak – cleared ground with nothing to burn on it – can often stop a bush fire in its tracks, but in a high wind, sparks and burning twigs can

easily cross the gap to restart the flames.

The Oshkosh eight-wheel fire truck is one of the world's most powerful appliances. Its two monitors can spew 190,000 liters (41,600 gal) of foam in 150 seconds. The Oshkosh weighs in at a hefty 60 tonnes (59 tons).

The world's biggest ambulances are four vehicles made in Belgium for taking handicapped people on trips across Europe. The Van Hool Jumbulances are 18 m (59 ft) long and can carry up to 44 patients and medical staff and their equipment.

Emergency technology

This glossary explains many of the technical terms used in this book.

Apparatus
Word used to describe any type of fire fighting vehicle, from a small hose tender to a large aerial ladder truck.

Centrifugal pump
Simple design used in many modern fire apparatus. In such a pump, fan blades spin around, sucking water up an inlet pipe and ejecting it with great force through an outlet pipe.

Damage control
Also known as salvage units. Crews working in salvage concentrate on limiting damage at fires by laying waterproof sheets, removing broken glass and protecting furniture. They also keep access passages clear and may remove valuables before they are damaged.

First-aid vehicle
Apparatus designed to get to a fire as rapidly as possible and start operations before the main fire brigade arrives. Carries basic equipment such as fire extinguishers, short ladders, axes and so on.

Foam pumper
Apparatus used in situations where water is not suitable, such as at airports, where most fires involve burning airplane fuel. Water sprayed on any oil-based liquid will simply spread the fire. Foam works by smothering the flames, as it contains carbon dioxide, a gas that deadens fire. The damp foam also cools the fire, reducing the chances of it starting again. Gas-powered dry powder sprays can also smother fires, laying a fine layer of chemical on the burning area. They don't cool the flames though, so are used only where there is little danger of a fire restarting.

Hydrant
Access point to the public main water supply. From here, fire fighters can connect a hose to the fire engine's pump. This draws water along the suction hose and through the pump itself. The water can then be either piped directly to a monitor or

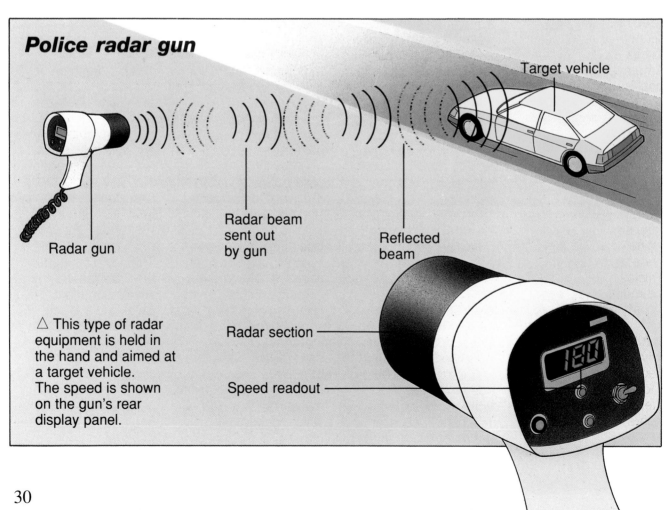

Police radar gun

Target vehicle

Radar gun

Radar beam sent out by gun

Reflected beam

Radar section

Speed readout

△ This type of radar equipment is held in the hand and aimed at a target vehicle. The speed is shown on the gun's rear display panel.

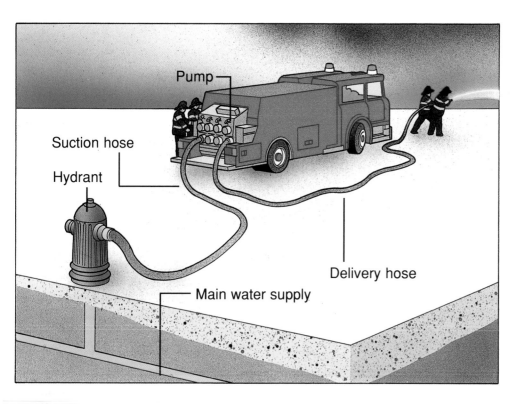

Pump

Suction hose

Hydrant

Delivery hose

Main water supply

Nobel peace prize in 1901 for his pioneering aid work. The Red Cross is matched in Islamic countries by the similar Red Crescent. The St. John's Ambulance Brigade is another voluntary organization, which works alongside official medical teams.

Smoke equipment
Breathing smoke or fumes is highly dangerous, so firemen often wear breathing masks and oxygen tanks to enable them to go into smoke-filled buildings. In several air crashes, passengers have died as a result of breathing poison fumes

through a delivery hose to a nozzle, held by fire fighters. Hydrants are often above-ground installations. Where access is below ground level, firemen may fix a stand pipe to the main water supply valve.

Internal-combustion (IC) engine
Engine in which fuel is burned inside . A steam engine uses an outside burner to heat a water-filled boiler to make steam. IC engines are used by almost all modern vehicles, from cars and motorcycles to trucks and buses.

Monitor
Swiveling nozzle, used to direct water or foam onto a fire. Often mounted on fire apparatus roofs or at the top of snorkels.

Motorized fire engine
Used to describe fire engines powered by an internal combustion engine. Smaller vehicles generally use car-type gasoline engines, while heavier ones are fitted with diesel engines.

Radar gun
Uses the same principle as radar used in aircraft. A radio beam is sent out by a transmitter. Objects in the way of the beam reflect it back as a radar "echo." The speed of the object (a road vehicle in the case of a radar gun) can be worked out by the length of time it takes for the echo to return. Gatso is a type of gun that can be set to register a difference in speed between two vehicles. Police officers cruising at a set speed can set

their Gatso to automatically take a picture of any vehicle overtaking faster than a set limit.

Rapid intervention vehicle (RIV)
Performs first-aid fire fighting at an airport. Typically, a light truck carrying basic equipment.

Red Cross
International society for the relief of suffering in times of war or disaster. Formed by Henri Dunant, who won the

given off by burning fabrics. Some major airlines are now planning to install smokehoods as a survival aid.

Squirt
Early type of fire extinguisher that looked like a bicycle tire pump. To use a squirt, the nozzle was placed in a bucket and water was sucked up when the plunger was pulled back. The squirt could then be aimed at a fire and water could be sprayed out.

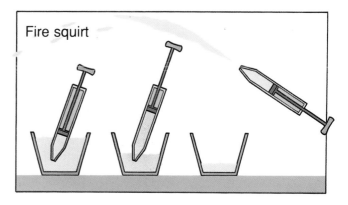

Fire squirt

Index

PRINTED IN BELGIUM BY

proost
INTERNATIONAL BOOK PRODUCTION